Healthy Family Meals & Snacks

Eat Better, and Feel Good from Dawn to Dusk

BY: Matthew Goods

Copyright © 2021 by Matthew Goods

Copyright Page

All rights remain reserved. This publication or any of its content may not be published, distributed, copied, or printed without the explicit permission or authorization of the author. No part of this book may be reproduced in any form, you may only use brief excerpts of the book in published reviews. This book is protected under the law. The author is not responsible or liable for any damage caused by the reader's use of this book.

Table of Contents

Introduction 6

    Butternut Squash Breakfast Hash 8

    Carrot Waffles 11

    Chai Spiced Granola 14

    Coconut Flour Pancakes 17

    Eggs Benedict 19

    Greek-Style Avocado Toast 22

    Sausage, Kale, and Parmesan Egg Muffins 24

    Smoked Salmon Frittata 27

    Strawberry and Rhubarb Chia Jam Overnight Oat Parfaits 30

    Toasted Coconut Quinoa Oatmeal 33

Snacks 35

    Avocado Deviled Eggs 36

    Baked Radish Chips 38

    Cauliflower Tots 40

    Four-Seed Crackers 43

Marinated Greek Yogurt Cheesy Balls 46

Peanut Butter Asian Lettuce Wraps 48

Rainbow Veggie and Cream Cheese Pinwheels 50

Roast Chickpeas 52

Spinach and Cottage Cheese Dip with Raw Veggies 54

Zucchini, Carrot, and Honey Muffins 56

Lite Bites & Mains 59

Baked Orange Chicken 60

Cauliflower Crust Marinara Pizza 63

Greek-Style Mac 'n Cheese with Roasted Garlic and Leeks 66

One Pot Chicken Stew 70

Slow Cooker Turkey Chili 73

Sticky Salmon with Tangerine Salad 76

Stuffed Pumpkin 79

Tomato and Two Cheese Tart 82

Whole Wheat Pasta Alfredo 85

Zucchini Lattice Lasagna 88

Desserts 90

Almond and Quinoa Blondies 91

Banana Split Pops 94

Chocolate Chia Pudding 96

Coconut-Chocolate Truffles 98

Fruit Cheesecake Bark 100

Grilled Pineapple 102

Oaty Apple Crumble 104

Peach FroYo 106

Skinny Strawberry Mousse 108

Zesty Lemon Squares 110

Afterword 113

About the Author 114

Introduction

One of the keys to unlocking health and happiness is to eat better. So if you want to embrace a healthy weekly meal plan and are looking for ways to feel well from dawn to dusk, check out our 40 sweet and savory recipes.

From lean protein to fiber-rich foods, these healthy meals and snack recipes provide all the tools you will need to eat better and feel good.

Eating better and enjoying a healthy and balanced diet is a vital part of ensuring well-being and can help you and your family feel your very best.

Doing this means eating protein and fiber-rich foods, fresh fruit and veggies, dairy products, dairy alternatives, and healthy fat.

What's more, eating better and feeling good involves avoiding ready-made meals and snacks that may be either high in fat or salt.

Check-out our best healthy 40 recipes, including breakfasts, lite bites, mains, snack, and desserts today!

Butternut Squash Breakfast Hash

Wake up to a healthy breakfast, get the day off to a flying start and enjoy this healthy hash.

Servings: 2

Total Time: 50mins

Ingredients:

- 1 tbsp extra-virgin olive oil
- 2 cups butternut squash (cubed)
- Sea salt and black pepper (to season)
- ⅓ cup scallions (chopped)
- 1 small zucchini (cut into 1" pieces)
- 1½ cups broccoli florets (chopped)
- 2 tbsp fresh rosemary (minced)
- 1 tsp balsamic vinegar
- 1 clove garlic (peeled and finely chopped)
- 3 kale leaves (stemmed and chopped)
- 2 pinches of smoked paprika
- 3-4 fried eggs

Directions:

Preheat the oven to 400 degrees F. Using parchment paper, line a large baking sheet.

In a large skillet over moderate heat, heat the olive oil.

Add the butternut squash along with a drizzle of olive oil, a pinch of salt, and a dash of pepper, and toss to combine. Roast the squash in the oven for 25-30 minutes, until golden.

To the pan, add the scallions, zucchini, broccoli florets, rosemary and a few pinches of salt, and a dash of black pepper. Cook for 6-8 minutes, until lightly golden brown.

Add the balsamic vinegar, garlic, roasted squash, and kale. Season once again with salt, black pepper, and a pinch of paprika. Sauté until golden brown, for around another 5 minutes, while occasionally stirring.

In a frying pan, fry the eggs to your desired level of doneness.

Top with fried eggs, and enjoy.

Carrot Waffles

Who doesn't love waffles for breakfast? And these warm carrot waffles served with a drizzle of sweet maple syrup and a dollop of coconut cream are pleasantly spiced and crisp.

Servings: 4-6

Total Time: 25mins

Ingredients

- 2 cups whole spelt flour
- 2 tsp baking powder
- 2 tbsp ground flaxseed
- ½ tsp nutmeg
- ½ tsp ground cinnamon
- Sea salt (to season)
- 1 cup carrots (trimmed and grated)
- 2 cups almond milk (room temperature)
- ¼ cup coconut oil (melted)
- 1 tsp vanilla extract
- 2 tbsp pure maple syrup
- Maple syrup (to serve)
- Coconut cream (to serve)

Directions:

Preheat a waffle iron.

Combine the flour with baking powder, flaxseed, nutmeg, cinnamon, and a pinch of salt in a bowl.

In a second bowl, combine the grated carrots with almond milk, coconut oil, vanilla extract, and maple syrup.

Fold the carrots into the flour mixture from Step 2, and stir until just combined.

Scoop an appropriate amount of waffle batter onto your waffle iron and cook until the waffles are slightly crisp.

Serve the waffles topped with maple syrup and a dollop of coconut cream.

Chai Spiced Granola

Nutritious and filling, this warmly spiced granola will keep you fuller for longer, staving off those mid-morning munchies.

Servings: 4-6

Total Time: 45mins

Ingredients:

- 2 cups almonds
- ¾ cup pecans
- ½ cup cashews
- 1 cup sunflower seeds
- 1 cup pumpkin seeds
- 1 tbsp cinnamon
- 1 tsp ginger
- 1 tsp cardamom
- ½ tsp allspice
- 2 tbsp blackstrap molasses
- ½ cup maple syrup
- 2 tsp vanilla extract

Directions:

Preheat your main oven to 275 degrees F.

In a food processor, pulse the nuts and seeds, one variety at a time, to a moderately fine texture but stopping before they become a butter. Add the mixture to a large bowl.

Add the cinnamon, ginger, cardamom, allspice, molasses, maple syrup, and vanilla extract, and with clean hands, mix fully to combine.

Using parchment paper, line 2 baking sheets.

Divide the granola mixture evenly between the sheets in a flat, single layer.

Place the baking sheets in the oven and bake for 10 minutes. Remove from the oven and stir. Rotate the pans and return to the oven. Cook for another 10-15 minutes, taking care not to burn.

Remove from the oven and set aside to cool for 30 minutes.

Serve and enjoy.

You can store any leftover granola in a sealed container.

Coconut Flour Pancakes

Coconut flour is high in protein and fiber, which adds extra nutritional value to this tasty breakfast. With some simple swaps like these, pancakes needn't be a treat reserved only for the weekend.

Servings: 1

Total Time: 30mins

Ingredients:

- ⅓ cup 2% Greek yogurt
- 2 tbsp maple syrup
- 2 tbsp butter (melted)
- 3 large eggs (separated)
- ⅓ cup coconut flour
- Pinch kosher salt
- ½ tsp bicarb of soda
- Nonstick cooking spray
- Honey and fresh fruit (for topping, to serve)

Directions:

In a large bowl, whisk together the yogurt, maple syrup, butter, and egg yolks. Add the coconut flour, salt, and bicarb of soda. Fold until combined.

In a second bowl, whip up the egg whites using an electric mixer until they can hold stiff peaks. Fold the stiff egg whites into the pancake batter until incorporated.

Spritz a large nonstick skillet with cooking spray and arrange over moderately low heat.

Spoon 2 tbsp of the pancake batter into the skillet and spread evenly. Cook for 1-2 minutes or until bubbles start to form. Flip the pancake and cook for another 1-2 minutes until golden and cooked through.

Repeat with the remaining pancake batter.

Serve the pancakes warm, drizzled with honey and fruit if desired.

Eggs Benedict

This healthy version of a breakfast or brunch classic is re-invented by switching English muffins for sweet potato toast. Meanwhile, Greek yogurt forms the basis of a creamy Hollandaise sauce.

Servings: 4

Total Time: 45mins

Ingredients:

- Hollandaise Sauce:
- 2 egg yolks
- 1 tsp Dijon mustard
- 5¼ ounces plain Greek yogurt
- 1 tbsp chives (snipped)
- Black pepper (to season)
- Eggs:
- 1 sweet potato (cut into ½"slices)
- 4 eggs
- 4 slices Canadian bacon
- Fresh parsley (chopped, to garnish)

Directions:

First, prepare the sauce: In a heatproof bowl, whisk the egg yolks with mustard and Greek yogurt. Set the bowl over a pan of just simmering water and cook for around 12-15 minutes while constantly stirring, until thickened. Fold in the chives, and season to taste with black pepper.

Remove the pan from the heat and keep warm while in the pan.

Preheat the main oven to 400 degrees F.

Arrange the sliced sweet potato on a baking sheet and bake in the oven until cooked through, for 30-40 minutes.

Once the potatoes are almost cooked, prepare the remaining ingredients.

In a frying pan, over moderate heat, cook the bacon for around 60 seconds on each side. Put aside.

Bring a pot of water to a simmer. Using a spoon, swirl the water to create a vortex. Crack the eggs into the water and poach for 3-4 minutes. Take the eggs from the pot and transfer to a bowl.

When the sweet potatoes are cooked, transfer them to plates. Top with the bacon, a poached egg, and a drizzle of yogurt and chive Hollandaise sauce.

Garnish with fresh parsley and enjoy.

Greek-Style Avocado Toast

A Californian healthy staple breakfast gets a Greek makeover with feta cheese and Kalamata olives. Kali Orexi!

Servings: 4

Total Time: 10mins

Ingredients:

- 2 avocados (pitted)
- ½ lemon
- Sea salt and black pepper
- A pinch of red pepper flakes
- 4 slices sourdough bread (toasted)
- ½ cup Greek feta (crumbled)
- ½ cup grape tomatoes (halved)
- ½ cucumber (chopped)
- ½ cup Kalamata olive (pitted and chopped)
- ¼ cup dill (chopped)
- Extra-virgin olive oil (to drizzle)

Directions:

Remove the avocado halves from their skin, and transfer to a bowl.

Squeeze some of the juice from the lemon over the avocado and season with salt, black pepper, and red pepper flakes. Using a fork, mash the seasoned avocado. Taste and adjust the seasoning if needed.

Spread the mashed avocado over the toasted sourdough bread and top with crumbled feta cheese, halved tomatoes, cucumber, olive, and chopped dill. Drizzle olive oil over the top and enjoy.

Sausage, Kale, and Parmesan Egg Muffins

Having a busy lifestyle is no excuse not to eat better. These delicious egg muffins are the perfect grab-and-go breakfast treat and, better yet, are packed with protein.

Servings: 12

Total Time: 40mins

Ingredients:

- 12 large eggs
- Salt and black pepper (to season)
- ½ pound Italian sausage meat
- 3 cups kale (roughly chopped)
- 1 shallot (diced)
- 1 cup Parmesan (grated)

Directions:

Preheat the main oven to 350 degrees F. Set aside a 12-hole muffin tin.

Add the eggs to a large cup, season with salt and black pepper, and whisk until fluffy. Set aside for the moment.

In a pan over moderate heat, sauté the sausage until just browned. While cooking, use a spatula to break up the sausage meat.

Next, add the kale and shallot to the pan. Sauté for 2 more minutes, or until the kale is wilted. Take the pan off the heat.

Spoon the sausage kale mixture into the muffin tin so that the holes are halfway full. Sprinkle a little Parmesan cheese into each hole. Pour the egg mixture into the muffin tin so that the holes are 90% full.

Place the muffin tin in the oven and bake for 20-25 minutes until cooked through.

Take the cooked muffins out of the oven and allow them to cool a little before removing them from the tin.

Enjoy straight away or keep stores in the refrigerator.

Smoked Salmon Frittata

This seafood frittata is dairy-free, but that doesn't mean that either taste or texture is compromised. It is healthy and makes the perfect breakfast or brunch dish to share with family or friends.

Servings: 6

Total Time: 40mins

Ingredients:

- 3 tbsp olive oil (divided)
- 1 leek (cleaned, with light green and white parts diced)
- 1 shallot (diced)
- 3 scallions (thinly diced)
- 10 large eggs
- 1 cup Greek yogurt
- A bunch of fresh parsley (coarsely chopped)
- A bunch of fresh dill (coarsely chopped)
- 8 ounces smoked salmon (torn into small pieces)
- 4 ounces goat cheese
- Salt and freshly ground black pepper (to season)

Directions:

In a 10"cast-iron skillet over moderate heat, heat 1 tablespoon of oil.

Add the leek, shallot, and scallions to the pan and sauté for 1-2 minutes, until just translucent. Remove the mixture to a plate and put to one side.

In a bowl, add the eggs and Greek yogurt, and whisk to combine. Next, stir in the parsley, dill, smoked salmon, goat cheese, sautéed leeks, shallot, and scallions. Season the mixture with salt and black pepper.

When the skillet has cooled down, wipe clean using a kitchen paper towel.

Over low heat, add 2 tablespoons of oil to the wiped skillet to make sure the bottom of the pan is coated fully.

Pour the egg mixture into the skillet and cook for around 8-10 minutes until the frittata's sides are just beginning to set.

Transfer the frittata to the middle shelf of the oven. Turn the top broiler on. Continue to cook for an additional 8-10 minutes, checking on it every 3 minutes to make sure the top isn't overly browning. If the frittata does cook faster than the inside, turn the broiler off and allow it to cook in the oven.

Serve the frittata and enjoy.

Strawberry and Rhubarb Chia Jam Overnight Oat Parfaits

Eating well is all about forward planning, and this overnight oat breakfast dish goes a long way towards feeling better and a healthy lifestyle.

Servings: 2

Total time: 9hours 20mins

Ingredients:

Strawberry Rhubarb Chia Jam:

- 2 cups strawberries (hulled and chopped)
- 1 cup rhubarb (trimmed and chopped)
- ½ tsp freshly squeezed lemon juice
- A pinch of salt (to season)
- 1½-2 tbsp maple syrup
- 2 tbsp chia seeds

Oats:

- 1 cup whole rolled oats
- 1 cup almond milk
- A pinch of salt (to season)
- Maple syrup (to drizzle)
- Granola (to serve)
- Coconut cream (to serve)

Directions:

First, prepare the jam. In a small pan over moderate heat, at a simmer, cook the strawberries, rhubarb, fresh lemon juice, and salt for 10 minutes while frequently stirring. Do not allow the fruit to stick to the bottom of the pan. Take the pan off the heat and stir in the maple syrup and chia seeds. Allow the mixture to cool to room temperature for 20-30 minutes.

Transfer the jam to a jar and allow to chill in the fridge for a minimum of 60 minutes

Next, prepare the oats. Divide the oats into 2 glass jars. Pour in the milk and add a pinch of salt and maple syrup to sweeten. Stir well to combine, cover and chill in the fridge overnight.

The following day, assemble the oat jars with a scoop of jam.

Top with granola, a drizzle of maple syrup, and a dollop of coconut cream.

Toasted Coconut Quinoa Oatmeal

Few things are more warming on a cold morning than a big bowl of creamy oatmeal. This toasted coconut porridge is scrumptious, but what's more, it is made with quinoa as well as oats. Quinoa is one of the few foods that contain all nine essential amino acids. Enjoying a satisfying breakfast will make it easier to avoid sugary snacks pre-lunchtime, something that is essential in any quest to eat better.

Servings: 4

Total Time: 30mins

Ingredients:

- 1 (14-ounce) can light coconut milk
- ½ cup quinoa
- A pinch of kosher salt (to season)
- 1½ cups rolled oats
- 1 cup water
- Ground cinnamon (to taste)
- ½ cup unsweetened toasted coconut flakes

Directions:

In a small saucepan over moderate heat, bring the coconut milk to a boil. Add the quinoa to the pan and season with a pinch of salt. Cook for 15 minutes or until the quinoa is cooked.

Add the oats, water, and pinch of cinnamon to the pan and stir to combine. Cook for 2-3 more minutes to soften the oatmeal.

Divide the oatmeal between serving bowls and garnish with toasted coconut flakes.

Snacks

Avocado Deviled Eggs

Eggs and avocado are a winning combination of good fats. Rich in protein, easy, and quick to prepare, this snack will satisfy all those hunger pangs.

Servings: 2

Total Time: 15mins

Ingredients:

- 6 eggs (hard-boiled)
- 1 ripe avocado (peeled and pitted)
- Freshly squeezed juice of 1 lime
- 2 tbsp red onion (peeled and finely chopped)
- 2 tbsp cilantro (finely chopped)
- 1 tsp garlic powder
- Salt and black pepper (to seasons)

Directions:

Cut the hard-boiled eggs in half and transfer the yolk only to a bowl. Place the white halves on a platter.

To the bowl of yolks, add the avocado, lime juice, onion, cilantro, garlic powder, salt, and black pepper. Using a fork, mash until combine and creamy.

Scoop up the mixture with a spoon and dollop it into the egg white halves.

Serve and enjoy.

Baked Radish Chips

Baked, not fried, these veggie chips are way better than the potato variety. What's more, they are deliciously served with Ranch dip.

Servings: 4

Total Time: 1hour 30mins

Ingredients:

- 7 medium radishes
- 1 tbsp canola oil
- ½ tsp garlic powder
- Salt and black pepper (to season)
- Ranch dip (to serve, optional)

Directions:

Preheat the main oven to 225 degrees F.

Using a veggie peeler, remove the red skins from the radishes. This step is optional. Leaving the skins on the radishes will give them a peppery flavor.

Next, with a mandolin, thinly slice the radishes, and transfer to a bowl.

Add the oil and garlic powder to the bowl. Season the radishes with salt and black pepper and toss to coat evenly.

Spread the radishes in an even layer on baking sheets, making sure that they don't overlap.

Bake in the oven for 1 hour 15 minutes, or until crisp and lightly golden. Allow to cool for 5 minutes before serving with ranch dip.

Cauliflower Tots

Grain and gluten-free, you can tuck into these cauliflower tots and enjoy some guilt-free snacking.

Servings: 6

Total Time: 1hour

Ingredients:

- 4 cups cauliflower florets
- 1 large egg
- ½ onion (peeled and grated)
- ¼ cup blanched almond flour
- ¼ cup Parmesan (shredded)
- ¼ cup Cheddar cheese (shredded)
- Sea salt and freshly ground black pepper (to season)
- Avocado oil cooking spray
- Ketchup (to serve, optional)

Directions:

Preheat the main oven to 400 degrees F. Using parchment paper, line a rimmed baking sheet.

Fill a pan with 1" of water, and bring to a boil. You need to be able to place a steamer basket over the pan.

Put the cauliflower florets in a steamer basket set over the pan of boiling water. Cover with a lid, and steam for 5 minutes, until fork-tender.

In batches, place the steamed florets in a food blender or processor and process until chopped into a meal consistency, for around 10 seconds. Transfer each batch of meal to a clean fine piece of cheesecloth. When all the meal is cool enough to hand, gather the corners of the cheesecloth, and while working over the kitchen sink, squeeze out as much liquid as possible. Place the squeezed cauliflower meal to a bowl.

Add the egg, grated onion, flour, cheeses, salt, and pepper to the bowl. Using a rubber spatula, mix the ingredients well to combine. Set the mixture aside to rest for 4-6 minutes until it comes together.

Spritz the parchment-lined baking sheet with avocado oil cooking spray.

Using clean hands, form the mixture into 34 small tater tots, approximately 1" long by ½" wide. Arrange the tots on the prepared baking sheet, around 1" apart. Spray the tots liberally with cooking spray.

Bake in the oven until golden brown, for around 20 minutes. Flip over and continue cooking for an additional 10 minutes until browned all over.

Season with more salt, and serve with a bowl of ketchup for dipping.

Four-Seed Crackers

Four types of seeds combine to create crunch crackers that are perfect for enjoying with beer, wine, or soda. Top with your favorite spread, with cheese, or on their own.

Servings: 8

Total Time: 3hours 10mins

Ingredients:

- ½ cup pumpkin seeds
- 1 cup ground flax seeds
- ⅓ cup sesame seeds
- ¼ cup chia seeds
- 1 tsp salt
- 1¼ cups water
- ½ tsp ground garlic
- ½ tsp ground onion
- 1 tsp dried thyme
- 1 tsp dried basil

Directions:

Preheat the main oven to 200 degrees F.

Add the pumpkin seeds to a food processor and pulse 6-8 times until they are a coarse sand consistency.

In a bowl, combine the coarse pumpkin seeds with flax seeds, sesame seeds, chia seeds, salt, water, ground garlic, ground onion, thyme, and basil. Stir well for 60 seconds until combined.

Set 2 (11x17") baking sheets and put to one side.

Place half of the mixture on a large sheet of parchment paper. Set a second sheet of paper over the top and roll to your preferred thickness. Repeat the process with the remaining half.

Take a knife, and score into even size pieces.

Place the parchment sheets with the cracker mixture onto the baking sheets and cook until dehydrated fully, for 2½-3 hours. Rotate the pans halfway through cooking.

Allow the crackers to completely cool, and break apart.

Marinated Greek Yogurt Cheesy Balls

The taste and texture of these balls are a cross between cream cheese and goat cheese and are perfect spread on crackers or crusty bread.

Servings: 8

Total Time: 48hours 10mins

Ingredients:

- 2 cups Greek yogurt
- ½ tsp salt
- 1 tsp za'atar seasoning
- Crackers or crusty bread (to serve)

Marinade:

- Olive oil (as needed)
- 1 tsp za-atar seasoning
- 1 tbsp fresh chives (chopped)

Directions:

In a bowl, combine Greek yogurt with salt and 1 teaspoon of za'atar seasoning.

Scoop the mixture into a piece of clean cheesecloth and tightly knot. Place the bundle into a mesh strainer set over a bowl. Set aside on your worktop, at room temperature, for 60 minutes. When this time has elapsed, drain the liquid that forms in the bowl, and transfer to the fridge for 1-2 days.

Take the strained Greek yogurt out of the cheesecloth and using clean hands form into 1 ounce balls.

Transfer the cheese balls to a Mason jar and pour in enough oil to fill, followed by 1 teaspoon of za-atar and chopped chives.

Place the jar in the fridge for 1 day.

Serve the cheese balls with crusty bread.

Peanut Butter Asian Lettuce Wraps

Asian-style food is ideal for snacking. It ticks so many boxes, taste, texture, presentation, and more.

Servings: 6

Total Time: 20mins

Ingredients:

- ⅓ cup reduced-sodium teriyaki sauce
- ¼ cup hoisin sauce
- 3 tbsp smooth and creamy peanut butter
- 1 tbsp rice vinegar
- 1 tbsp sesame oil
- 1½ pounds lean ground turkey
- ½ cup carrot (trimmed and shredded)
- 2 tbsp fresh ginger root (peeled and minced)
- 4 cloves garlic (peeled and minced)
- 1 (8-ounce) can whole water chestnuts (drained and chopped)
- ½ cup fresh snow peas (chopped)
- 4 green onions (chopped)
- 12 Bibb lettuce leaves

Directions:

In a bowl, whisk the teriyaki sauce, hoisin sauce, peanut butter, rice vinegar, and sesame oil.

In a large frying pan, cook and crumble the ground turkey with the carrot over moderately high heat, until no pink remains, for 6-8 minutes. Drain the meat, and add the ginger and garlic. Cook while stirring for 60 seconds.

Stir in the sauce mixture, water chestnuts, peas, and onion, and heat through.

Spoon the mixture into lettuce leaves, and serve.

Rainbow Veggie and Cream Cheese Pinwheels

Snacking needn't be unhealthy, and these colorful pinwheels will help get you through the day.

Servings: 4-8

Total Time: 20mins

Ingredients:

- ⅔ cup reduced-fat whipped cream cheese
- 1 tbsp dry ranch powder
- 4 large tortillas
- ½ cup red bell pepper (cut into thin strips)
- ½ cup carrot (trimmed and cut into thin strips)
- ½ cup yellow bell pepper (cut into thin strips)
- ½ cup baby spinach leaves
- ½ cup purple cabbage (shredded)
- 1 cup cooked chicken (shredded)

Directions:

In a bowl, combine the cream cheese with the ranch powder until combined fully.

Spread the cream cheese mixture evenly over the tortillas. Leave a 1" border all the way around. In 2 tablespoonful amounts lay the red bell pepper, carrots, yellow bell pepper, baby spinach leaves, and purple cabbage in rows across the tortillas. Top with cooked and shredded chicken.

Roll each tortilla up tightly. If the ends don't remain closed, add a dot more of cream cheese to seal.

Cut the pinwheels crosswise and serve.

Roast Chickpeas

Chickpeas aren't solely for making hummus, and this pop-in-the-mouth snack is crunchy, spicy, and super satisfying.

Servings: 4

Total Time: 55mins

Ingredients:

- 1 (15-ounce) can chickpeas (drained and rinsed)
- 1 tbsp vegetable oil
- ½ tsp sea salt
- Seasoning:
- 1 tsp cumin
- 1 tsp chili powder
- ½ tsp dried oregano

Directions:

Preheat the main oven to 350 degrees F.

Spoon the chickpeas in an even layer onto a baking sheet.

Place the baking sheet in the preheated oven and roast for 8-10 minutes, until entirely dry.

Remove the chickpeas from the oven and toss with vegetable oil and sea salt.

Return the baking sheet to the oven and bake for 30-35 minutes, until dry and crisp, tossing halfway through roasting.

On a sheet dry, combine the chickpeas, cumin, chili powder, and dried oregano, and toss to evenly combine. Spread into an even layer and allow to cool completely.

Store the roasted chickpeas in a ziplock bag.

Spinach and Cottage Cheese Dip with Raw Veggies

Avoid those blood sugar crashes by snacking on foods rich in protein. Good sources of this are eggs, seeds, yogurt, and of course, cottage cheese.

Servings: 4

Total Time: 8mins

Ingredients:

- 1 bunch spinach (stalks removed, rinsed, patted dry and chopped)
- ⅓ cup fresh mint leaves
- ½ cup reduced-fat cottage cheese
- 2 tsp freshly squeezed lemon juice
- 1 tsp garlic (peeled and minced)
- Salt and freshly ground black pepper (to season)

Crudites:

- A bunch of carrots (peeled, and cut into batons)
- 1 small bunch radishes (trimmed and halved)
- 7 ounces raw green beans (ends trimmed)
- 4 ounces fresh whole baby corn

Directions:

First, add the spinach to a food blender or processor. Add the mint, cottage cheese, fresh lemon juice, and minced garlic. Process until combined and thickened. Transfer the mixture to a bowl and season with salt and black pepper.

Serve the spinach and cottage cheese dip with raw carrots, radishes, green beans, and baby corn.

Zucchini, Carrot, and Honey Muffins

Pop these tasty veggie muffins in your lunchbox and enjoy them as a mid-morning snack. We guarantee your co-workers will want you to share!

Servings: 12

Total Time: 35mins

Ingredients:

- 1 medium zucchini (grated)
- 1 carrot (trimmed, peeled, grated, and divided)*
- 1 shallot (finely chopped)
- ½ cup Cheddar cheese (grated)
- 2 cups self-raising flour
- 3 organic eggs
- ¼ cup olive oil
- 1 cup yogurt
- ¼ cup runny honey (divided)
- Salt and black pepper (to season)
- 2 tbsp fresh cilantro leaves (chopped)

Directions:

Preheat the main oven to 375 degrees F. Grease a 12-cup muffin pan.

Add the zucchini and ¾ of the grated carrot to a large bowl. To the bowl, add the shallot, grated cheese, and flour and stir well to incorporate.

In a second bowl, whisk eggs, olive oil, plain yogurt, and 2 tablespoons of honey, and add to the zucchini mixture. Season the mixture with salt and black pepper. Add the cilantro and mix thoroughly to combine.

Evenly divide the mixture between the 12 muffin cups, and top with the remaining carrot. Drizzle over the remaining honey and bake in the oven until firm to the touch and golden, for 15-20 minutes.

Remove from the oven allow to stand while in the pan for 4-6 minutes. Transfer the muffins to a wire baking rack and allow to cool.

Serve and enjoy.

*Grate the carrots on the large holes of a grate and grate into long strands.

Lite Bites & Mains

Baked Orange Chicken

Forget deep-frying and instead opt for baked chicken. It is just as tasty and way better for you.

Servings: 4

Total Time: 40mins

Ingredients:

- 2 cups all-purpose flour
- 2 large eggs (beaten)
- 2 cups panko breadcrumbs
- 1 pound skinless, boneless chicken breasts (cut into chunks)
- Salt and freshly ground black pepper (to season)
- ⅓ cup reduced-sodium soy sauce
- Fresh juice and zest of 2 oranges
- ¼ cup honey
- 2 cloves garlic (peeled and minced)
- 2 tsp fresh ginger (peeled and freshly grated)
- 2 tbsp cornstarch
- 2 cups jasmine rice (cooked)
- Sesame seeds (to garnish)
- Green onions (sliced, to garnish)

Directions:

Preheat the main oven to 400 degrees F. Using parchment paper, line a baking sheet.

Add the flour to one shallow bowl, and the eggs to a second, the breadcrumbs to a third,

Dredge the chicken first in the flour, then coat in beaten egg, and finally cover with breadcrumbs. Season the chicken with salt and black pepper.

Next, prepare the sauce. Combine the soy sauce, orange juice, honey, garlic, ginger, and cornstarch in a small pan over moderate heat. Whisk well until incorporated and cook for around 5 minutes, until thickened.

Transfer the chicken to a bowl, and toss in the orange sauce, to coat.

Serve the baked orange chicken over rice, garnish with orange zest, sesame seeds, and sliced green onions.

Serve and enjoy.

Cauliflower Crust Marinara Pizza

If pizza is your favorite, but you aren't so keen on overloading on the carbs, then this cauliflower crust makes a great alternative.

Servings: 4

Total Time: 50mins

Ingredients:

- Sea salt (to season)
- 1 large head cauliflower (trimmed, cored, and coarsely chopped)
- 1 large egg
- 2 cups mozzarella (shredded and divided)
- ½ cup Parmesan (freshly grated and divided)
- Nonstick cooking spray
- ¼ cup marinara style sauce (of choice)
- 2 cloves garlic (peeled and minced)
- 1 cup grape tomatoes (halved)
- Fresh basil (torn, to serve)
- Balsamic glaze (to serve)

Directions:

Preheat the main oven to 425 degrees F.

In a large frying pan, bring approximately ¼" of water to a boil and season with sea salt.

Add the cauliflower in an even, single layer and cook until crisp-tender for 3-4 minutes.

Transfer to paper towels and squeeze gently to remove any excess water.

Add the drained cauliflower to a food blender and process on pulse until grated. Drain the excess water in kitchen paper towels.

Transfer the drained cauliflower to a bowl and add the egg, 1 cup mozzarella, and ¼ cup Parmesan. Season the mixture with salt.

Spritz nonstick cooking spray over a baking sheet.

Transfer the 'dough' to the baking sheet and pat to create a crust. Bake in the oven for 20 minutes and until dried out.

Spoon the marinara sauce over the crust, followed by the remaining mozzarella and Parmesan, garlic, and tomatoes, and bake until the crust is crisp and the cheeses melt. This step will take another 10 minutes.

Garnish the pizza with basil and drizzle over balsamic glaze.

Serve and enjoy.

Greek-Style Mac 'n Cheese with Roasted Garlic and Leeks

They say the Mediterranean diet is one of the world's healthiest ways of eating. If you are preparing a meal for family or friends, when you serve this Greek-style dish, there is no need to compromise your eat better, feel well meal plan.

Servings: 4-6

Total Time: 2hours 35mins

Ingredients:

Mac 'n Cheese:

- 3 tbsp butter (divided)
- 1 tbsp + 3 tsp olive oil (divided)
- ½ sweet onion (peeled and chopped)
- 1 leek (trimmed and thinly sliced)
- 1 head of garlic
- 1 pound rigatoni
- 1 cup fresh baby spinach (chopped)
- 1 tsp flour
- ⅔ cup milk
- ⅓ cup heavy cream
- 1 tsp oregano
- ½ tsp rosemary
- 1 cup Asiago cheese (shredded)
- 11 ounces feta cheese in brine (crumbled)
- ½ cup sun-dried tomatoes (chopped)
- ½ tsp black pepper

Directions:

Preheat the main oven to 400 degrees F.

In a pan, heat 2 tablespoons of butter and 1 teaspoon of olive oil until the butter melts.

Add the onion and leeks to the pan, and stir until evenly coated. Reduce the heat to its lowest setting and cook while stirring every 10 minutes, for 60 minutes until golden. Remove the pan from the heat and put to one side.

Slice the top ¼ off the garlic head. Drizzle the remaining oil over the top of the garlic, and wrap in aluminum foil. Roast the garlic in the oven for half an hour. Remove from the oven, and allow to cool completely before squeezing the garlic from its peel.

Preheat your oven to the lowest setting.

Cook the pasta according to the package instructions and until al dente. Drain, strain, and drizzle a drop of oil over the pasta, shaking to combine. Doing this will prevent the pasta from sticking to itself.

In a frying pan, heat 1 tablespoon olive oil, and sauté the spinach until wilted. Remove and put aside.

Heat the remaining butter in a pan over low heat until it melts.

Whisk in the flour until incorporated fully.

Pour in the milk and heavy cream and continue to heat until not boiling but hot.

Add the oregano and rosemary and mix thoroughly.

Next, add the asiago cheese and crumbled feta. Stir the mixture until the feta is starting to melt.

Remove the pan from the heat. In a 13x9" baking dish, combine the cheese mixture with the drained pasta, spinach, tomatoes, onions, leeks, and roasted garlic. Season with black pepper, and place in the preheated broiler for 6-10 minutes, until the tips of the pasta are browned lightly.

Serve!

One Pot Chicken Stew

If you are feeling under the weather or in need of a little comfort, then this family chicken stew is the recipe for you. Serve with chunks of crusty bread and enjoy.

Servings: 6-8

Total Time: 1hour

Ingredients:

- 1 tbsp ghee
- 1½ pounds lean chicken breast (cubed)
- 4 cups potatoes (cut into cubes)
- 1 onion (peeled and diced)
- 3 carrots (trimmed, peeled, and chopped)
- 4 celery stalks (trimmed and chopped)
- 1 tbsp tapioca starch
- 1 tsp salt
- ½ tsp black pepper
- ½ tsp paprika
- A pinch of thyme
- 4 cups chicken stock
- 1-2 tbsp full-fat coconut milk
- Crusty bread (to serve)

Directions:

In a large Dutch oven, set over moderate heat, heat the ghee.

When hot, add the cubes of chicken and cook for 6-8 minutes until browned. Take the chicken out of the pan, and put to one side.

To the pan, add the potatoes, onion, carrots, and celery. Sauté for 8-10 minutes until the veggies begin to soften.

Return the chicken to the pan and add the tapioca starch, salt, black pepper, paprika, and thyme. Cook the mixture for another 2 minutes.

Pour in the chicken stock and bring the mixture to a boil. Turn the heat down and simmer for 20-30 minutes until the liquid has reduced slightly and the mixture has thickened.

Add a splash of coconut milk, and serve.

Slow Cooker Turkey Chili

Comforting and good for you, what's not to love about this low-protein chili? Serve with brown rice for a healthier option.

Servings: 8

Total Time: 4hours 20mins

Ingredients:

- 1 tbsp extra-virgin olive oil
- 1 red onion (peeled and finely chopped)
- 1 green bell pepper (chopped)
- 1½ pounds ground turkey
- Sea salt and freshly ground black pepper (to season)
- 2 cloves garlic (peeled and minced)
- 2 tbsp tomato paste
- 2 (14-ounce) cans chopped tomatoes
- 1 (15-ounce) can black beans (rinsed and drained)
- 1 (14½-ounce) can kidney beans (rinsed and drained)
- 1½ cups reduced-sodium chicken broth
- 2 tsp chili powder
- 1 tsp ground cumin
- 1 tsp dried oregano
- Cheddar cheese (shredded, to garnish)
- Green onions (thinly sliced, to garnish)

Directions:

In a large frying pan, over moderately high heat, heat the oil.

Add the red onion and bell pepper, and cook until it starts to soften, for around 4 minutes.

Add the ground turkey and cook while occasionally stirring until the turkey is golden but not entirely cooked through. Season the meat with salt and black pepper and stir in the garlic and tomato paste. Cook the mixture for 2-3 minutes, until fragrant. Transfer to a slow cooker.

To the slow cooker, add the tomatoes, black beans, kidney beans, broth, chili powder, cumin, and oregano. On high, cook for 4 hours until the chili has thickened. Taste and season with salt and black pepper.

Garnish with shredded cheese and sliced green onions.

Serve and enjoy.

Sticky Salmon with Tangerine Salad

This lite bite to share is colorful, flavorful, packed with lots of healthy ingredients, and 100 percent good for you.

Servings: 2

Total Time: 15mins

Ingredients:

- 2 (5-ounce) skinless salmon fillets
- 2 tsp organic honey
- Salt and freshly ground black pepper (to season)
- 2-3 tbsp mixed seeds
- 4 tangerines
- 1 tbsp extra-virgin olive oil
- 1 tbsp red wine vinegar
- 1¾ ounces watercress
- 8¾ ounces vinegar-free cooked beetroot (drained and cut into thin wedges)

Directions:

Preheat the main oven to 390 degrees F.

Brush each fish fillet lightly with half of the honey, and season with black pepper. Then, press on the mixed seeds.

Transfer the fish to a baking sheet, and bake for around 15 minutes, depending on the thickness of the fillets, until cooked through and seeds are crunchy.

In the meantime, peel the tangerines and cut into segments. Set any juice that is released from the fruit to use for the dressing.

Add the juice to a jug or small bowl, and whisk in the olive oil, red wine vinegar, and a little salt and black pepper.

Add the watercress, beetroot, and tangerine segments to a bowl. Add the dressing and toss to combine.

Top the dressed salad with the salmon and enjoy.

Stuffed Pumpkin

Serve this stuffed pumpkin straight from the oven. It makes an impressive centerpiece for a Thanksgiving spread or Halloween party and is sure to be a big hit with non-meat eaters.

Servings: 4

Total Time: 1hour 15mins

Ingredients:

- 1 (2.2 pounds) medium fresh pumpkin
- 4 tbsp extra-virgin olive oil (divided)
- 3½ ounces wild rice
- Zest and juice of 1 lemon
- 1 Bramley apple (cored and thinly sliced)
- 1 fennel bulb (thinly sliced)
- 1 tbsp fennel seeds
- ½ tsp red chili flakes
- 2 cloves garlic (peeled, minced, and divided)
- 1 ounce toasted pecans (coarsely chopped)
- 1 large handful of fresh parsley (coarsely chopped),
- Salt and freshly ground black pepper (to taste)
- 3 tbsp tahini
- Pomegranate arils (to garnish)

Directions:

Preheat the main oven to 390 degrees F.

Cut the top off the pumpkin, and with a metal spoon, scoop out the seeds. Remove end discard any pith. Keep the top of the pumpkin to use as a 'lid.' You can either discard the seeds or use them for another recipe.

Place the pumpkin on a baking sheet, and rub all over, inside and out, with 2 tablespoons of olive oil. Season the pumpkin well and roast in the middle of the oven until fork-tender, to 45 minutes. Also, place the 'lid' of the pumpkin to the side.

Meanwhile, rinse the rice and cook according to the package directions. Finally, spread the cooked rice out on a baking tray and set it aside to cool.

Squeeze half the lemon over the diced apple and fennel to prevent them from discoloring.

In a frying pan, heat the remaining oil.

Add the fennel seeds and chili flakes to the pan, and fry until they start to pop. Stir in half of the garlic and the sliced fennel. Cook for 5 minutes until softened before stirring in the apple, pecans, and lemon zest. Remove the pan from the heat, and add the mixture to the cooked rice. Fold through the chopped parsley, and season to taste with salt and black pepper.

Pack the mixture into the cooked pumpkin and return to the hot oven. Cook for around 10-15 minutes, until hot.

In the meantime, whisk the remaining lemon juice with the tahini, remaining garlic, and sufficient water to create a dressing consistency.

Top the pumpkin with pomegranate arils and dressing.

Cover with the 'lid' and serve from the table.

Tomato and Two Cheese Tart

Nutrient-rich cottage cheese is high in protein, minerals, and B vitamins. It can help to boost muscle and is a highly beneficial food to add to your weekly meal plan.

Servings: 6-8

Total Time: 1hour 5mins

Ingredients:

- 1 (9") frozen store-bought pie shell
- 3 pounds ripe, medium-size tomatoes
- ¼ cup fresh basil (finely sliced)
- Salt and freshly ground black pepper (to season)
- 1 cup full-fat cottage cheese
- ½ cup Monterey Jack cheese (shredded)
- ½ cup Swiss cheese (shredded)
- ¼ cup mayonnaise

Directions:

Preheat the main oven to 350 degrees F.

Place the pie shell on a baking sheet and bake in the preheated oven for a few minutes, browned gently for around 10 minutes. Remove from the oven and put to one side. Do not turn the oven off.

Cut the tomatoes in half, and squeeze each half to remove the juice and seeds. Slice the tomatoes and layer them in the prebaked pie shell. Scatter over the basil between the layer, and season to taste with salt and black pepper.

In a bowl, combine the remaining ingredients (cottage cheese, Monterey Jack cheese, Swiss cheese, and mayonnaise). Spread the mixture over the tomatoes and bake in the oven until the cheese melts and is golden, for around 45-50 minutes.

Take the pie out of the oven and allow to stand at room temperature.

Slice into wedges.

Serve and enjoy.

Whole Wheat Pasta Alfredo

All it takes is a few simple tweaks to transform a calorific Alfredo into a healthy main meal. Skip the cream and instead use Greek yogurt, and use whole wheat linguine as your chosen carbohydrate.

Servings: 4

Total Time: 30mins

Ingredients:

- 12 ounces whole-wheat linguine
- 1 tbsp extra-virgin olive oil
- 3 cloves garlic (peeled and minced)
- 2 tbsp all-purpose flour
- 1 cup reduced-sodium chicken broth
- ¾ cup 1% milk
- ½ cup Parmesan (grated)
- 2 tbsp Greek yogurt
- Salt and black pepper (to season)
- A pinch of crushed red pepper flakes
- Fresh parsley (chopped, to garnish)

Directions:

Bring a large pot of salted water to a boil. Add the linguine and cook according to the package directions, and until al dente. Drain, and put aside ½ cup of pasta cooking water. Put the drained pasta to one side, until needed.

In a frying pan, over moderate heat, heat the oil. Add the garlic to the butter, and sauté for 60 seconds until fragrant.

Scatter the flour evenly over the top, and stir to combine. Cook the mixture until it is lightly golden in color.

A little at a time, in 2 tablespoonful amounts, add the broth while whisking until entirely smooth between additions.

Bring the mixture to a boil, and slowly stream in the milk while whisking. Bring to a simmer and cook for 2-3 minutes, until the sauce is thickened.

Remove the pan from the heat, and add the grated cheese and Greek yogurt. Season to taste with salt, black pepper, and a pinch of red pepper flakes.

Add the cooked and drained pasta along with ¼ cup of the reserved pasta water to the sauce, and toss to combine evenly. If the sauce is too thick, add a little more water in one tablespoonful amounts until you achieve your preferred consistency.

Garnish with chopped parsley and serve.

Zucchini Lattice Lasagna

If you are a fan of traditional lasagna, why not give this low-carb meat-free version a try?

Servings: 8-10

Total Time: 1hour

Ingredients:

- 2 cups ricotta
- 1 cup Parmesan (freshly grated)
- 2 eggs
- Sea salt and black pepper (to season)
- 1½ cups marinara sauce (store-bought)
- 3 zucchini (cut into wide strips and drained on kitchen paper)
- 3 cups mozzarella (shredded)

Directions:

Preheat the main oven to 350 degrees F.

In a bowl, combine ricotta with grated Parmesan, and eggs. Season the mixture with sea salt and black pepper.

Spread a thin layer of the marinara sauce in a casserole dish, and add 2 layers of zucchini noodles followed by the zucchini noodles, ricotta-egg mixture, and mozzarella cheese.

Finally, create a zucchini lattice. Layer the noodles side by side in a diagonal in the dish. Lift the bottom half of every other noodle, and lay another noodle diagonally across. Repeat the process until the top layer is full.

Scatter over more grated Parmesan and season well with salt and black pepper.

Bake until the cheese is melted and the zucchini is cooked through, for around 30 minutes.

Allow to rest for 8-10 minutes before serving.

Desserts

Almond and Quinoa Blondies

These soft, nutty blondies are made using quinoa flour, an ingredient you can find in your local health food store, making these bakes gluten-free. Limiting gluten intake can contribute to improved gut health, so incorporating more recipes like this one into your diet is a great step towards eating better.

Servings: 24

Total Time: 1hours 35mins

Ingredients:

- Nonstick cooking spray
- ¾ cup natural almond butter
- ¼ cup unsalted butter (at room temperature)
- 2 large eggs
- 1 tsp vanilla extract
- ¾ cup brown sugar
- ¾ cup quinoa flour
- ¼ tsp salt
- 1 tsp baking powder
- 1 cup semi-sweet chocolate chips

Directions:

Preheat the main oven to 350 degrees F. Line an 8" square baking tin with parchment paper. Spritz nonstick cooking spray.

Using an electric mixer, beat together the almond butter and unsalted butter until creamy. Next, beat in the eggs, vanilla, and brown sugar.

In a separate bowl, combine the quinoa flour, salt, and baking powder. Add the dry ingredients to the wet and mix until combined.

Fold the chocolate chips into the batter.

Pour the blondie batter into the prepared baking tin.

Place in the oven and bake for approximately 30 minutes or until golden. Take the blondies out of the oven and allow them to rest in the tin for 45 minutes.

Lift the blondies out of the pan and cut into squares.

Allow to cool completely before serving.

Banana Split Pops

Eating better does not mean giving up on your favorite treats but simply finding new healthier ways to enjoy them. These banana split pops are a lighter way to enjoy all the delicious flavors of a classic banana split.

Servings: 8

Total Time: 2hours 30mins

Ingredients:

- 4 ripe bananas (peeled, halved crosswise)
- 1 tbsp coconut oil
- 1¼ cups chocolate chips
- ½ cup rainbow sprinkles
- Light whipped cream (to serve)

Special Equipment:

- 8 popsicle sticks

Directions:

Cover a large cookie sheet with wax paper.

Insert a popsicle stick into each banana half and arrange on the prepared cookie sheet. Place in the freezer for 2 hours.

Add the coconut oil and chocolate chips to a microwave-safe bowl. Cook in the microwave, in 30-second intervals, stirring often until melted.

Add the sprinkles to a shallow bowl.

Dip each frozen banana halfway into the chocolate and then into the sprinkles to coat evenly.

Return the pops to the cookies sheet and freeze for another 15 minutes until the chocolate is set.

Top each banana pop with a small dollop of whipped cream before serving.

Chocolate Chia Pudding

Chia seeds are a fantastic ingredient to include in your meals if you are trying to eat better; they are rich in antioxidants, fiber, minerals, and fatty acids. What's more, they give an irresistibly thick texture making this chocolate pudding both yummy and filling.

Servings: 2

Total Time: 4hours 20mins

Ingredients:

- 2 tbsp cocoa powder
- 1 tsp vanilla extract
- 2 tbsp maple syrup
- 1 cup almond milk
- ¼ cup chia seeds
- Fresh raspberries (to garnish)
- Coconut flakes (to garnish)

Directions:

In a medium bowl, stir together the cocoa powder, vanilla extract, maple syrup, almond milk, and chia seeds to combine. Set aside for 15 minutes.

Stir the mixture and then cover with plastic wrap, chill for 4 hours.

Divide the chia pudding between serving bowls and garnish with fresh raspberries and coconut flakes.

Enjoy!

Coconut-Chocolate Truffles

Rich, fudgy, and decadent, you would never guess these chocolate and coconut truffles are free from refined sugar and dairy! Vegan and paleo-friendly, these truffles will satisfy a chocolate craving while still nourishing your body.

Servings: 10-12

Total Time: 40mins

Ingredients:

- ¾ cup almond butter
- ½ cup coconut cream
- 2 tbsp coconut oil
- 1 cup cocoa powder
- ½ cup coconut sugar
- ¼ tsp vanilla extract
- ¼ tsp salt
- Coconut sugar (as needed, for rolling)

Directions:

In a medium saucepan over low heat, melt together the almond butter, coconut cream, and coconut oil. Stir until silky and combined.

Take off the heat, add the cocoa powder, coconut sugar, vanilla, and salt, stir to combine.

Transfer to the refrigerator for half an hour.

Roll the mixture into even size balls and then roll each truffle in coconut sugar to coat.

Store the truffles in the refrigerator until ready to eat.

Fruit Cheesecake Bark

Made with protein-rich Greek yogurt and low-fat cream cheese, this fruity cheesecake bark is far healthier than it tastes.

Servings: 6

Total Time: 6hours 15mins

Ingredients:

- 2½ cups 2% Greek yogurt
- 6 ounces low-fat cream cheese (at room temperature)
- Pinch kosher salt
- ¼ cup honey
- 1 tsp vanilla extract
- ½ cup raspberries
- ¼ cup fresh blueberries
- ⅓ cup strawberries (hulled, sliced)
- ¼ cup graham crackers (crushed)

Directions:

Cover a baking sheet with parchment paper.

Add the yogurt and cream cheese to a bowl and, using a hand mixer, beat until fluffy. Next, add the salt, honey, and vanilla extract, beat again to combine.

Pour the mixture onto the baking sheet and smooth it into an even ½" thick layer.

Scatter the fruit and crushed graham crackers over the bark.

Transfer to the freezer for 4-6 hours until completely set. Break into shards before serving.

Grilled Pineapple

Fresh pineapple is flavored with aromatic spices and sweetened with coconut sugar before being grilled to sweet, sticky goodness. Serve with creamy coconut yogurt for a deliciously guilt-free dessert.

Servings: 6-8

Total Time: 20mins

Ingredients:

- 3 tbsp coconut sugar
- 1 tsp ground cardamom
- 2 tsp ground cinnamon
- 1 pineapple (peeled, cored, cut into ½" rings)
- Coconut yogurt (to serve)

Directions:

Preheat the grill to moderately low heat.

Combine the coconut sugar, cardamom, and cinnamon in a small bowl. Sprinkle ½ tsp of the mixture on each side of the pineapple rings. Place on the grill and cook for 3-4 minutes on each side until caramelized and golden brown.

Transfer to serving bowls and serve with coconut yogurt.

Oaty Apple Crumble

Cinnamon spiced apples sit beneath an oaty crumble topping for a warm and comforting dessert. What's more, with less than 180 calories per serving, you can enjoy this tasty treat guilt-free.

Servings: 6

Total Time: 30mins

Ingredients:

- 3 tbsp coconut oil (melted, divided)
- 3 cups apples (peeled, cored, chopped)
- 1 tsp ground cinnamon
- 1½ tbsp brown sugar
- 1 cup oats
- 1 tbsp maple syrup

Directions:

Preheat the main oven to 400 degrees F.

In a pan over moderate heat, melt 1 tbsp of the coconut oil. Add the apple and cook for 5 minutes until softened. Next, add the cinnamon and brown sugar, cook for another 2 minutes.

Transfer the cooked apples to a baking dish.

In a medium bowl, combine the oats with the remaining coconut oil and maple syrup. Scatter the mixture over the apples.

Place in the oven and bake for 20 minutes until golden.

Serve warm.

Peach FroYo

Eating better is all about making small, smarter decisions that add up to make a big difference. Swap peach ice cream for peach frozen yogurt, which is far lower in fat and sugar but still just as refreshing and delicious.

Servings: 6

Total Time: 10mins

Ingredients:

- 1 pound frozen chopped peaches
- ½ cup non-fat plain yogurt
- 4 tbsp honey
- 1 tbsp lemon juice
- Mint leaves (to garnish)

Directions:

To a food processor, add the frozen peaches, yogurt, honey, and lemon juice. Process for 4-5 minutes until smooth and creamy.

Serve the fro-yo straight away garnished with a fresh mint leaf.

If you are not ready to serve immediately, transfer to an airtight container and keep in the freezer for up to 1 month.

Skinny Strawberry Mousse

This air-light strawberry mousse gets a skinny makeover with the help of some unexpected ingredients like tofu and apple juice.

Servings: 6

Total Time: 4hours 20mins

Ingredients:

- 1 cup unseweetened apple juice
- ¼ cup cornstarch
- ⅓ cup honey
- ⅛ tsp kosher salt
- 1⅔ cups soft silken tofu (drained)
- 2½ cups fresh strawberries (hulled, chopped)

Directions:

Add the apple juice, cornstarch, honey, and salt to a saucepan over moderate heat. Stir to combine and bring to a simmer.

Turn the heat down a little and continue to simmer for 30-40 seconds.

Take the pan off the heat and allow to cool for 10 minutes; the mixture should be very thick.

Add the cooled apple mixture to a food processor along with the tofu and strawberries. Blitz until smooth and creamy.

Pour the mixture into 6 (6-ounce) serving dishes or ramekins. Transfer to the refrigerator and chill for at least 4 hours before serving.

Zesty Lemon Squares

If you favor tart, citrusy desserts, then these zesty lemon squares are the perfect option for you. A crumbly whole wheat crust is the perfect base for a creamy, melt-in-the-mouth lemon curd topping.

Servings: 16

Total Time: 5hours 15mins

Ingredients:

Crust:

- ¾ cup whole-wheat flour
- ⅓ cup coconut oil
- ¼ tsp kosher salt
- ¼ cup maple syrup

Topping:

- 6 eggs
- 4 tsp lemon zest
- ⅓ cup honey
- ½ cup fresh lemon juice
- 4 tsp coconut flour
- ¼ tsp kosher salt

Directions:

Preheat the main oven to 350 degrees F. Line an 8" square baking tin with parchment paper.

Prepare the crust. Combine the flour, coconut oil, salt, and maple syrup. Mix well until combined. The mixture should have a shortbread-like consistency. Press the mixture evenly into the prepared baking tin.

Bake the crust in the oven for 20 minutes until lightly browned. Take out of the oven and allow to cool.

In the meantime, prepare the topping. Beat together the eggs, lemon zest, honey, lemon juice, coconut flour, and salt until smooth. The mixture will be runny.

Pour the topping over the cooled crust. Bake for half an hour.

Take out of the oven and allow to cool completely. Chill for 4 hours before slicing into squares and serving.

Afterword

You finished this book and read it all to this point. To be honest, there's no way I can show you how much I appreciate you. You took the time out of your very busy life to stare at my thoughts that I put into words, thank you. You've already done enough but I still have one more favor to ask of you, feedback. I would love to know what you think about this book's content; did you enjoy it? Was it worth your time? Do you have any suggestions for future books? I'm open to comments and I'll love to hear from you.

Thank you again

Matthew Goods

About the Author

Known as the boy wonder of Homemade cuisine, he has been dubbed the "Jack of all Spices". Born in a small town in South Carolina, Matthew Goods was a local boy who, at a very early age of 7 had found a hobby that will stick with him for the rest of his life in the culinary arts. He loved being in and around the kitchen whenever his mother late.

This meant Matthew spent most of his free time after school alone, and he filled this time by experimenting with different mixes, ingredients, and spices and by the time he was 15, he was already a budding chef at one of the best-rated restaurants in the town. After traveling around the world for over a decade, working at various levels of restaurants, Goods now runs a successful restaurant that serves his special recipes where he is the executive chef.